The Equator

Written by
Angie Belcher

T0364492

Contents

Collins

What is the Equator?

If you look closely on a globe, you will observe the line of the Equator.

People navigate using this imaginary line that goes around the middle of the earth.

the Equator

Andes mountains

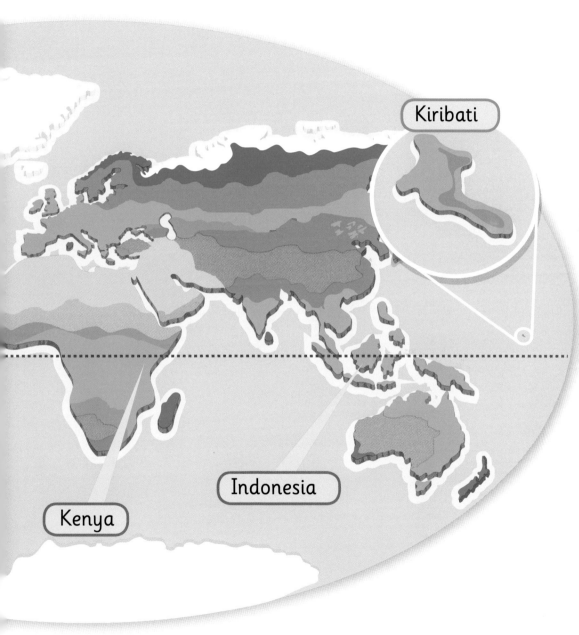

Kiribati

Indonesia

Kenya

3

What is the weather like?

The earth bulges in the middle which means the land along the Equator is closest to the sun.

The weather is extremely hot, and the heat makes rain clouds so it's also very wet.

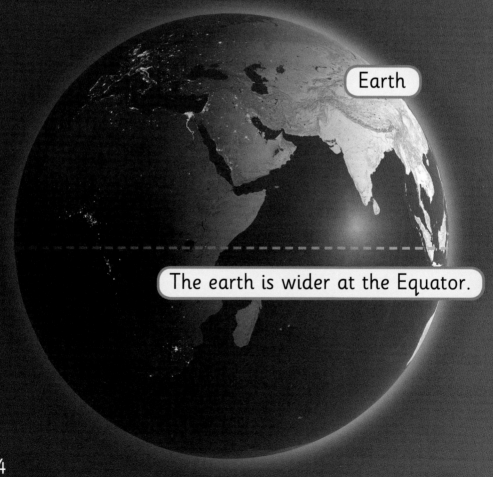

Earth

The earth is wider at the Equator.

sun

In the dry season, the land becomes parched and crops don't grow.

When the heavy rain arrives, the rivers overflow and wash everything away.

What is the geography like?

The Equator crosses 14 territories ranging from snow-capped mountains to huge sand dunes.

The dry

In the dry heat of Kenya, wildlife migrates across the land looking for food and drink.

The people that follow and hunt the wildlife use skin and dung to construct houses.

Plants hold moisture in their leaves, whilst creatures like the bat-eared fox have developed large ears to keep them cool.

bat-eared fox

13

The wet

Dense rainforests grow in the wet, humid atmosphere of Indonesia.

Tall trees stretch up to the sunlight, while pitcher plants trap and eat insects.

pitcher plant

Strange creatures such as the chameleon have evolved bright colours, while heavyweight orangutans and monkeys swing from vines.

The high and the low

In the high Andes mountain ranges, people weave clothes from alpaca wool.

alpaca

In the low-lying atolls of Kiribati, shelters jut out into the sea to catch cooling breezes.

Shelters on stilts stay cooler.

The extreme weather makes life hard along the Equator, but people, plants and wildlife have found ways to adapt.

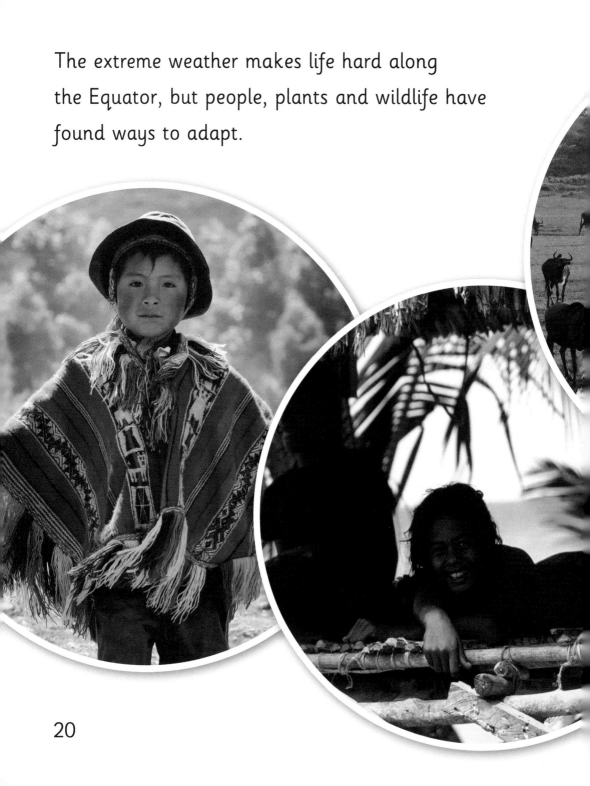

Extremes on the Equator

snow-capped mountains

huge sand dunes

dry heat

wet, humid atmosphere

After reading

Letters and Sounds: Phase 5

Word count: 303

Focus phonemes: /ai/ eigh a /igh/ y /ee/ y e e-e ey /ch/ tcht /c/ ch t /w/ wh /l/ le /j/ g ge /f/ ph /v/ ve /z/ se /s/ se

Common exception words: of, to, the, into, their, people

Curriculum links: Geography: Locational knowledge, Human and physical geography

National Curriculum learning objectives: Spoken language: articulate and justify answers, arguments and opinions; Reading/Word reading: apply phonic knowledge and skills as the route to decode words, read accurately by blending sounds in unfamiliar words containing GPCs that have been taught, read other words of more than one syllable that contain taught GPCs, read aloud accurately books that are consistent with their developing phonic knowledge; Reading/Comprehension: understand both the books they can already read accurately and fluently … by: drawing on what they already know or on background information and vocabulary provided by the teacher

Developing fluency

- Your child may enjoy hearing you read the book. Model reading with lots of expression.
- You may wish to take turns to read a page.

Phonic practice

- Help your child to get quicker at reading multi-syllable words. Ask them to:
  - Read the sounds in each syllable 'chunk' and blend.
  - Then read each chunk to read the whole word.

terr/it/or/ies	territories
ex/treme/ly	extremely
i/mag/in/a/ry	imaginary
ge/og/ra/phy	geography

  - Now read the words quickly without chunking them up.

Extending vocabulary

- Ask your child to spot the synonyms below. Which is the odd one out?

wet	parched	dry	(*wet*)
strange	huge	unusual	(*huge*)
swing	trap	capture	(*swing*)